BOOM AND BUST
Financial Cycles and Human Prosperity

To Griff —
great to see you

BOOM AND BUST
Financial Cycles and Human Prosperity

Alex J. Pollock

today and best wishes,
Pollock

AEI Press
Publisher for the American Enterprise Institute
Washington, D.C.

Cover image shows Marriner Eccles, Chairman of the Federal Reserve Board, during rapid-fire questioning at a committee meeting in 1939. This photograph symbolizes the intellectual and physical exhaustion imposed on responsible officials by financial crises.

Distributed by arrangement with the National Book Network
15200 NBN Way, Blue Ridge Summit, PA 17214
To order call toll free 1-800-462-6420 or 1-717-794-3800.

For all other inquiries please contact AEI Press, 1150 17th Street, N.W., Washington, D.C. 20036 or call 1-800-862-5801.

LCCN: 2010020471
ISBN-13: 978-0-8447-4383-7
eISBN-13: 978-0-8447-4384-4

CONTENTS

1

NOTHING NEW UNDER THE FINANCIAL SUN

"About every ten years, we have the biggest crisis in 50 years."

—*Paul Volcker, Former Chairman of the Federal Reserve*[1]

Most people know virtually no financial history, so when we have a financial crisis, it seems like it has never happened before. But it has.

The financial panic of 2007–09, with its massive losses revealed, displays the classic patterns of recurring credit cycles. In the bubble that preceded the panic, housing prices and mortgage borrowing rose to unsustainable heights and then crashed back to earth. Millions of mortgage borrowers ended up owing more on their homes than the properties were worth. The housing wealth that people thought they had fell by about $7 trillion. Defaults on mortgages soared. As the crisis deepened and spread beyond the housing sector, a serious recession ensued. The stock market lost more than half its value. Famous banks failed or had to be acquired by competitors able to absorb their losses. Governments in the United States and many other countries scrambled to design huge bailouts. Some journalists deluded themselves into thinking they were witnessing the "death of capitalism."

It was so dramatic that people might be forgiven for believing it was unique. But in historical perspective, we should not be surprised by these travails. We don't even have to look very far back for another bubble. Only ten years before, as the potential of the Internet became widely realized, the stock market prices of "dotcom" companies rose giddily over several years to spectacular heights, only to go bust in equally spectacular fashion, and a recession followed. In the bursting of the "Dotcom

Bubble," the technology stock index lost nearly two-thirds of its value and almost a decade later still trades at only half its bubble peak.

So, the United States, in succeeding decades, had first the equity bubble and bust of the 1990s and then the housing bubble and bust of the 2000s. Japan, in the 1980s, had a simultaneous equity and housing bubble and bust.

Bubbles are the unsustainable increase in the price of some asset (houses, most recently) that people end up buying because they believe the price will continue to rise. So, indeed, it does—for some time, perhaps several years, strengthening the belief. But when accompanied by large increases in borrowing, bubbles are unfailingly followed by crises, in which borrowers default, lending firms collapse, and the asset prices rapidly fall.

Let's look a little further back in the lessons of financial history.

> The [banking] failures for the current year have been numerous, many having been characterized by gross mismanagement and some by criminality....The unfavorable conditions were greatly aggravated by the collapse of unwise speculation in real estate.[2]

The words above read as though they could have been written in 2009 or 2010, as the banking failures of these years were indeed numerous and aggravated by unwise real estate speculation. In fact, these words were penned by the Comptroller of the Currency—the regulator of national banks—in 1891.

In 1912, soon-to-be-president Woodrow Wilson said, "Waiting to be solved...lurks the great question of banking reform."[3] Nearly a century later, it still seems to be lurking, and banking reform is once again widely debated.

With the creation of the Federal Reserve System, "financial or commercial crises seem to be mathematically impossible."[4] At least, that was what the Comptroller of the Currency mistakenly argued in 1914.

In 1922, at the beginning of the 1920s boom, then–Secretary of Commerce Herbert Hoover launched the government's "Own Your Own Home" campaign, which, among other things, encouraged mortgage loans. Mortgage debt greatly expanded in the 1920s. In 1927, the Congress significantly liberalized the terms on which national banks could make real estate loans, encouraging them to make more. The result? By 1932, Jesse Jones—who later became the formidable head of the Depression-era bailout operation, the Reconstruction Finance Corporation—observed, "Strewn all over was the wreckage of the banks which had become entangled in the financing of real estate promotions and had died of exposure to optimism."[5]

It is the professional duty of bankers and debt investors to be skeptical, not optimistic, but this seems to be forgotten in each financial cycle. As economist Abram

Piatt Andrew wrote in 1908: "The American panic of 1907...gave the lie directly to those who in recent years have contended that we should never again witness the experiences like those remarkable years 1837, 1857, 1873, and 1893."[6] All of these were years of financial crises.

Financial crises keep happening. The economic historian Charles Kindleberger, surveying three centuries of financial history, concluded that there has been a crisis about every ten years—the same estimate given by Paul Volcker in the earlier quote. "Kindleberger identified no fewer than thirty major financial crises in various countries between 1720 and 1990."[7]

More recently, the International Monetary Fund identified 88 banking crises in numerous countries around the world during the last four decades.[8] Of course, crises often occur in multiple countries at the same time. In a 2009 book, Carmen Reinhart and Kenneth Rogoff report 250 defaults by governments on their debt since 1800. Their compilation of banking crises in countries ranging from Albania to Zimbabwe is forty-five pages long.[9]

My own banking career began during the "credit crunch" of 1969. This was followed in 1970 by the bankruptcy of the giant Penn Central railroad—a "systemically important" railroad—which triggered panic in the commercial paper market, which, in turn, was bailed out by the Federal Reserve. The Penn Central railroad was then nationalized.

FINANCIAL EVENTS & CRISES

1900

PANIC OF 1907

1910

CREATION OF FEDERAL RESERVE

WORLD WAR I

1920

1920S BRIEF DEPRESSION / BOOM

FLORIDA LAND BOOM / BUST

STOCK MARKET PANIC
1930 INTERNATIONAL DEBT DEFAULTS
GREAT DEPRESSION
NATIONWIDE WIDE BANKING PANIC
RECONSTRUCTION FINANCE CORPORATION

1940

WORLD WAR II

1950

POSTWAR GROWTH & BULL MARKET

1960

CREDIT CRUNCH OF 1966

CREDIT CRUNCH OF 1969
1970 BANKRUPTCY / NATIONALIZATION
OF PENN CENTRAL RAILROAD
FIRST OIL SHOCK / STOCK MARKET CRASH
REAL ESTATE BUST
GREAT INFLATION / STAGFLATION

1980 SAVINGS & LOAN INDUSTRY CRISIS

INTERNATIONAL DEBT CRISIS
OIL & ENERGY BUBBLE / BUST
GOVERNMENT BAILOUT OF FARM CREDIT SYSTEM
SAVINGS & LOAN INDUSTRY COLLAPSE
1990 COMMERCIAL REAL ESTATE BUST

MEXICAN, ASIAN, & RUSSIAN DEBT CRISES
DOTCOM BUBBLE / BUST
2000

HOUSING BUBBLE
RUN ON NORTHERN ROCK BANK
MORTGAGE BUST; FAILURE OF FANNIE MAE, FREDDIE MAC, LEHMAN, AIG
FINANCIAL PANIC
2010 LIVING IN THE WAKE OF THE BUBBLE

In 1974 and 1975, a massive real estate bust occurred. About two-thirds of bank loans to real estate investment trusts—the enthusiasm of the day—were nonperforming (that is, borrowers could not make their loan payments). The Senate Banking Committee held hearings on what then-chairman William Proxmire called the "inordinate risk to the banking system."[10] Indeed, had banks been forced to write down their loans (that is, formally account for those loans' reduced value) to what they could be sold for in the debt market at that point, the entire banking system probably would have become insolvent.

Less than a decade later, the series of crises that marked the 1980s began with the default of Mexico on its foreign debt in 1982, which spread to a global crisis in loans to developing countries. The 1980s also included the collapse of the highly regulated savings and loan industry (financial institutions that specialize in home mortgage loans), which had a taxpayer bail-out costing about $150 billion. Then there was another terrific commercial real estate bust, and the failure of more than 1,400 highly regulated commercial banks in the decade, not to mention the government bailout of the Farm Credit System.

Adding together the U.S. commercial banks and the savings and loans, more than 2,200 failed between 1982 and 1992. Citibank—a huge and famous bank then as now—was in deep trouble, and it was not alone. The headline "Banks Entering Era of Painful Change—More Bailouts, Bankruptcies, Layoffs Likely," seemingly taken from 2009, was published in July 1991.[11] That same month, a Wall Street author penned this remarkable line: "Lenders are unlikely to repeat their past mistakes."[12] But, of course, they did, and generated the next crisis.

In an even longer view, the basic idea of cycles appears in the book of Genesis, Chapter 41. This is Pharaoh's dream of the seven fat cows and the seven lean cows, which Joseph rightly interprets as seven good years followed by seven bad years.

What is the lesson? Financial cycles inevitably accompany economic life. But so does the continued upward progress of living standards and national wealth in a market economy. Notwithstanding numerous financial crises, people today live better than their parents, far better than their grandparents, and vastly better than their more distant ancestors. They live longer, are healthier, eat better, are better educated, work in less dangerous and arduous jobs, more easily afford basic necessities, and have more choices and wider horizons. As Warren Buffett, the best-known investor of our time, wrote about the most recent crisis:

> Never forget that our country has faced far worse travails in the past. In the 20th century alone, we dealt with two great wars...a dozen or so panics and recession; virulent inflation which led to a 21.5% prime rate in 1980; and the Great Depression of the 1930s.... In the face of these obstacles—and many others—the real standard

of living for Americans improved nearly seven-fold during the 1900s.[13]

In other words, on average over time, the trend is for greater and greater overall economic well-being. While bubbles and crises continue, we cycle around a rising trend. This is because free markets release the energy of enterprise, entrepreneurship, application of new knowledge, and investment in new and better products and ways of producing them. The trend in the graph of constant purchasing power of U.S. gross domestic product per capita since 1900 is quite clear.

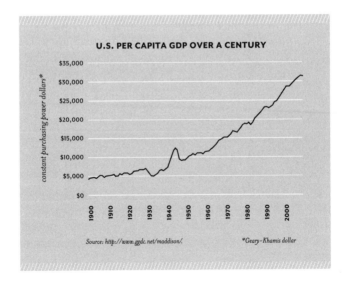

U.S. PER CAPITA GDP OVER A CENTURY

Source: http://www.ggdc.net/maddison/.   **Geary-Khamis dollar*

However, the energy of innovation is also disruptive. Over time, the economic well-being of average people keeps increasing in a most remarkable way, but we also have cycles and crises. The long-term trend is the good news. In a celebrated phrase of his great 1776 book, *The Wealth of Nations*, Adam Smith called this trend of increasing economic well-being "the natural progress of opulence."[14] Can we have the wonderful trend without the cycles? No, we can't. The next chapter explains why.

2

**THE DISTURBING
EXPERIENCE OF
WATCHING YOUR
FRIENDS GET RICH**

Human judgment, we know all too well, is fallible. People tend to get overexcited about the latest breakthrough, even though the breakthrough may be real, like the Internet. Even if the breakthrough becomes a permanent, scene-changing part of the economy, people enthusiastically overestimate, overbuild, overborrow, and otherwise make mistakes. There is no way to fix this problem, because the future is unknowable. There is no way for government or any other authority to decide in advance which innovations will succeed and which not, and to what extent. The only test is the marketplace, which arrives at the correct answer over time through a process of experimentation. Because of the inescapable limitations of human nature and of what the human mind is capable of predicting and knowing, we often overreact spectacularly in the short run—hence the recurring financial cycles.

In 1873, the insightful financial thinker Walter Bagehot[15] wrote a classic book on banking called *Lombard Street* (referring to the nineteenth-century London equivalent of "Wall Street"). The following passage from this book cannot be reread too often by those wishing to understand financial cycles:

> The mercantile community will have been unusually fortunate if during the period of rising prices it has not made great mistakes. Such a period naturally excites the sanguine and the ardent; they fancy that the prosperity they see

will last always, that it is only the beginning of a greater prosperity. They altogether [and all together] over-estimate the demand.... They all in their degree—and the ablest and cleverest the most—work much more than they should, and trade far above their means. Every great crisis reveals the excessive speculations of many houses which no one before suspected, and which commonly indeed had not begun or carried very far those speculations, till they were tempted by the daily rise of price and the surrounding fever.[16]

This was true when published in 1873, is true now, and will be true in the future. Bagehot's insights should have to be read and signed each year by all officers of financial firms, before they sign their required annual ethics statements. For, as Bagehot also pointed out, "The mistakes of a sanguine [optimistic] manager are far more to be dreaded than the theft of a dishonest manager."[17] Were the financial actors just stupid? No. It is essential to understand that this is not a problem of a lack of intelligence: as Bagehot says, "the ablest and the cleverest the most" get themselves in trouble. This was notably true of the brilliant Wall Street bankers and mathematical model builders who helped inflate and then were trapped in the deflation of the twenty-first-century bubble.

As a bubble expands, the belief in the ever-rising price of the favored asset seems to be confirmed by success on all sides. As long as the asset price keeps rising, everybody makes money. This strengthens the belief and helps keep the bubble inflating. With house prices rising rapidly for years, everybody—borrowers and lenders, brokers and investors, speculators and house flippers, home builders and home buyers, bond rating agencies and bond salesmen, realtors and municipalities, and many others, notably politicians—seemed to be winning.

Because so many people are making money from them while they last, bubbles are notoriously hard to control. One psychological element of bubbles is captured by this striking thought: There is nothing so disturbing to one's well-being and judgment as to see a friend get rich. Even worse is to see your brother-in-law get rich! The previously conservative investors get to feeling that they are suckers to miss out. They decide that they want a piece of the action.

Getting a piece of the action often means borrowing money—and if the price of an asset is always rising, more borrowing to buy it always seems better. From the lenders' point of view, loan experience is good during a bubble. Reported profits and prices of financial stocks are high. Loan delinquencies, defaults, and losses are all low. This seems to confirm the success of the credit expansion and the lenders' skills. For example, at the top of the housing bubble in 2005 and 2006, there were zero bank failures in the United States.

The defaults, losses, and failures all came later.

What if financial history were more widely studied, so

that really smart bankers also had historical perspective? Could universal knowledge among financial actors of this instructive history change the recurring bubble and bust behavior? Perhaps, but it is probably a utopian suggestion. Those who remember the crisis get old and pass from the scene; new generations arise to repeat the same mistakes.

Free, naturally flawed people making decisions in markets make mistakes. So do the naturally flawed people who make up government bureaucracies, including financial regulators and central banks. (As chapter 7 will discuss, government action both helped cause the twenty-first-century housing bubble and made it worse.) While the dynamism and innovation of market economies engender recurring financial bubbles and crises, they more importantly contribute to the trend of increasing human well-being. Economic cycles are not like roller coasters that go up and down but always return to the same place. Rather they are part of a broad trend line that, overall, continues to rise. It is easy to choose innovation, enterprise and a long-term growth trend, even with these financial cycles, over centrally planned stagnation.

3

ALL TOO HUMAN

Despite their historical frequency, the busts at the end of the bubbles take people by surprise. Then they ask the same questions. How did it happen? How did prices get out of control? How did so many risky loans get made? Who is guilty? What can we do so it never happens again?

The experience of a bubble is insidious. For a long while, from 2000 to 2006, the bubble generated profits and wealth. As prices rose, borrowers made more money as they bought houses on credit (often committing little or none of their own money); flippers bought and sold condominiums for a quick profit. Banks and other lenders benefited from interest and fees and paid big bonuses. Real estate brokers earned commissions. Investors in financial companies saw the market price of their stock investments rise. Home builders enjoyed a rush of new building. Home owners saw the values of their properties rise, seeming to bestow on them new wealth they could borrow against with home equity loans. State and local governments could collect higher property taxes on houses with higher assessed values. Investment banks packaged together mortgages into "mortgage-backed securities" and "collateralized debt obligations" that could be sold on international financial markets, and in the process earned very large profits. The bond-rating agencies were paid fees to rate mortgage-backed securities and were also highly profitable. Not least, politicians trumpeted and took credit for increasing home ownership and greater "access" to loans. The credit expansion was profitable for everybody involved—or so it seemed.

As long as the asset prices keep rising, the more people borrow, the more money everyone makes. Yet, much of the money everybody is making is coming from the expansion of risk and from the inflation of bank balance sheets. These increasingly have more debt compared to equity capital, which is called "increased leverage." The higher its leverage, the more money a bank seems to be earning, but the more it stands to lose if more loans than expected turn bad. The risk of losing outcomes is growing greater and greater.

There is nothing wrong with borrowing and lending in themselves—indeed, credit markets are essential to the functioning of any sophisticated economy.[18] Borrowing allows most people to own their own houses, many to own their own businesses or farms, companies to build new facilities, and governments to build new parks and roads. It is an over-optimistic excess of borrowing that causes trouble. Too much dedicated to buying bubble assets will end in disaster.

THE "MINSKY MOMENT"

In a famous remark of a century ago, philosopher George Santayana wrote that "Those who cannot remember the past are condemned to repeat it." The fact that the pattern of bubbles and busts keeps recurring, even though financial systems have been through it dozens of times before, suggests that there is something inside the system that produces bubbles.

The work of Hyman Minsky—a theorist of the human

foundations of credit bubbles and busts—is regularly rediscovered in times of financial crisis. The most recent crisis was no exception, with some even calling it a "Minsky Moment."

According to Minsky, busts do not result from some external force or shock to the financial system but rather are "endogenous"—that is, they arise from the intrinsic nature of human financial behavior. He writes, "Acceptable financing techniques are not technologically constrained; they depend upon the *subjective preferences and views* of bankers and businessmen."[19] In other words, the key factors that determine what can and cannot be done in financial markets are not mathematical or technical. Rather, loans and other financial transactions are made or not made based upon people's willingness to make a deal.

The key point is "subjective preferences." Those preferences determine whether an investment is viewed as risky and dangerous or normal and acceptable. These judgments change with time. Minsky continues: "Success breeds a disregard of the possibility of failure; the absence of serious financial difficulties over a substantial period leads to the development of a euphoric economy."[20]

In slogan form, Minsky's theory is that "stability creates instability." Or, in the words of the first-century Roman historian Velleius Paterculus, "The most common beginning of disaster was a sense of security."

David Simpson writes that, as the economy entered the twenty-first-century bubble, "Disinflation helped to usher in a feeling of confidence, first amongst policymakers and later amongst financial market participants, that a new and permanent era of financial stability and economic well-being had been achieved."[21] In 2004, Simpson continues, "Ben Bernanke, future chairman of the Federal Reserve Board, gave a speech entitled 'The Great Moderation'.... [H]e argued that modern macroeconomic policy had solved the problem of the business cycle."[22] Obviously, it hadn't.

Such optimistic positions are expected by Minsky's theory. Writing in 1986, Minsky noted that "As a previous financial crisis recedes in time, it is quite natural for central bankers, government officials, bankers, businessmen, and even economists to believe that a new era has arrived. Cassandra-like warnings that nothing basic has changed...are naturally ignored."[23]

The general pattern of bubbles and crises thus does not change, because the underlying human nature that drives them does not change. Whether calculations of boundless future profit opportunities from increasing leverage are made with quill pens or supercomputers, human behavior remains the same. As Charlie Munger of Berkshire Hathaway asked a decade ago, "How could economics not be behavioral? If it isn't behavioral, what is it?"[24] Or, as James Grant concluded from his study of the 1880s Kansas land bubble, "[I]n order to create a really big asset price bubble, a critical mass of human beings is all that's required."[25]

4

PANIC

Bubbles always end, and when they do, they tend to end in panics.

In bubbles, as we have seen, borrowing often expands dramatically. One perverse effect of bubbles is that, because in the expansion phase of the boom, few people default on their loans or are slow to make their payments, the whole system seems robust, and more lending is encouraged.

For many investors, not only banks, the amount of their borrowing relative to equity (their own money), their "leverage," rises. We see this in a basic way when home buyers come to have smaller and smaller down payments, and bigger and bigger mortgages, relative to the price of the house. In mortgage market jargon, this means the "loan-to-value ratio," or "LTV," gets higher.

The rapidly increasing availability of debt tends to push asset prices higher as people spend what they have borrowed, until the ability to repay the debt becomes dependent on the ability to sell the bubble asset at a higher price to somebody else (a so-called greater fool). The greater fool must be able to borrow still more to buy in turn. The system is now, in Minsky's term, "fragile."

What happens next is a panic.

Essential to understanding a panic is the role of very risk-averse short-term lenders. Short-term lenders are, put simply, investors who want their money back in a day, a week, or a month rather than years—they want the option of retrieving their money quickly, even if they have no immediate plans to do so. They range from bank depositors to investors in money market funds to interbank money market dealers (banks who make daily loans to other banks). Short-term lenders are not trying to make large profits. Rather, they seek a safe way to earn a modest return. These lenders are conservative and risk-averse.

Panics begin when these risk-averse lenders realize that, contrary to their intentions, their investments are at serious risk of loss. The realization is usually triggered by the financial difficulties or insolvency of some previously respected market actor: for example, in 2008, Bear Stearns, an investment bank, or Countrywide Financial, a big mortgage bank.

The short-term lenders' fears are compounded as asset prices begin to fall. Everyone starts to think about how low prices might go, instead of how high they will go. They focus on which other financial firms might collapse. They realize that they do not really know who is solvent and who is broke. They decide the first priority is to be safe.

The result: the short-term lenders all become even more conservative at once. They withdraw their money when its short term is up, and decline to make further loans. They seek the safety of Treasury bills—short-term debt issued by the U.S. government that are considered the safest investments possible. Treasury bills may pay little or even no interest in a panic, but they do keep the invested money safe. Investors have reached the moment described so well by the humorist Will Rogers: They no longer care about the return on capital, but about the return *of* capital.

The classic example of a panic is a bank run, when depositors—suspecting that their bank may soon fail—*rush all together* to withdraw their money. When this happens, any bank will fail. A famous fictional bank run occurs in the movie *It's a Wonderful Life*, in which George Bailey (Jimmy Stewart) has to explain to his customers that there is not enough cash in the bank to go around, since almost all of it has been lent out to them to buy their houses. In the real world of 2007–08, there was a similar, but much bigger, problem: an international run on mortgage and short-term debt markets. All the lenders wanted their money back at the same time.

Deposits in banks are not inherently stable—just the opposite. When depositors ask for their money back, banks are required to return it. Moreover, depositors generally have little or no knowledge of how sound their particular bank may be. Hence, when they sense trouble, their rational reaction is simply to protect their investment. This unavoidable logic has caused governments to provide "deposit insurance," which is really a taxpayer guaranty of bank deposits, so depositors don't have to run.

But large investors are not, and should not be, protected by such formal guarantees. The retreat of these investors from the short-term debt market poses a survival problem for banks and other financial firms, who depend on that money to cover their near-term obligations. Desperate for cash and unable to borrow, they have to sell assets in order to raise money. They have to sell in markets in which prices are falling—and the prices will be driven still lower by the rush of many firms trying to sell in order to raise cash. These are "distressed sales."

As financial firms lose money on distressed sales, their stability and solvency are further called into question, making it even more difficult for them to borrow. Short-term lenders become even less willing to make new loans or to renew existing ones amidst the general fear and heightened uncertainty about who is broke and who is not.

Meanwhile, many owners of the bubble asset find that its falling market price becomes less than the amount they owe on their loan. Remember that the inflation of the bubble is predicated on rising asset prices making the loans feasible. Once prices are falling, those borrowers who do not have the cash to make the required payments on their loans will often be unable to sell the asset for enough to cover what they owe. As this becomes widely understood, other creditors sense that a general collapse may be coming and rush to collect on their own investments while they still can.

As described two centuries ago by the great economist David Ricardo: "On extraordinary occasions, a general panic may seize the country, when every one becomes desirous of possessing himself of the precious metals [today's Treasury bills]—against such panic banks have no security on *any system*."[26]

Or, as Federal Reserve Chairman Bernanke said in 2009 in more academic terms: "Liquidity risk management at the level of the firm, no matter how carefully done, can never fully protect against systemic events…. In a sufficiently severe panic, funding problems will almost certainly arise and are likely to spread in unexpected ways."[27]

"LIQUIDITY" AND THE PLANK CURVE

The panic is caused by many investors and lenders becoming super-conservative and risk-averse all at once. Large bank and investing institutions, as well as individual investors, try to protect themselves by avoiding risk. The result is, ironically, to increase the risk that the financial system will cease to function. "Liquidity" disappears.

"Liquidity" is a financial term that refers to the ready availability of money. The term suggests there is some substance that could "flow," could be a "flood," could "slosh around," or could be "pumped" somewhere (to use a number of common expressions). But financial liquidity is not a substance. In good times, liquidity is abundant; it bad times, it disappears. What is it, then?

The puzzling, but true, answer is that it is verbal shorthand or a figure of speech to summarize the following financial market situation: A is ready and able to buy an asset from B on short notice, at a price that B considers reasonable. It can do this because C is willing to lend money to A. This means that C believes that A is solvent and that the asset is good collateral. Both A and C must believe that the asset could readily be sold to D. This also means that A and C believe there is an E willing to lend money to D.

It is apparent that liquidity in a financial market represents a complex set of relationships. It is really about group belief in the solvency of other parties (including banks) and the reliability of prices. During a boom, financial actors are confident that they know how well other institutions are doing, and what the right prices of financial assets are. They are much more willing to buy and sell, borrow, and lend. Assets change hands freely and frequently; liquidity is said to be abundant. During a crisis, these same financial actors do not know what assets are worth or which other firms are solvent or broke. They may not even know whether their own firm is solvent or broke. They become fearful and risk-averse. Liquidity has vanished.

Imagine a game of "musical chairs," with 500 players and 600 chairs. Leisurely music is playing, and every player finds it easy and natural to find a chair when needed. Suddenly, the music becomes frantic, and 200 chairs disappear. Now there are 500 players and 400 chairs: a wild scramble for chairs ensues, but 100 players fail to get one and are declared losers and out. But they each take a chair away as they go, so there are now 400 players and 300 chairs, and more frantic music and scrambling. This pattern continues. "Liquidity" is the belief that you can always get a chair, and liquidity has now disappeared.

This dynamic can be summarized in more formal terms by the Plank Curve, which represents the amount of liquidity in the market as a function of uncertainty and fear. The name of the curve derives from its resemblance to the path of a man walking the plank.

The point of this chart is that liquidity disappears

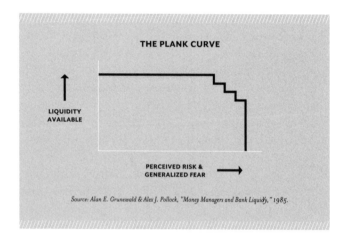

THE PLANK CURVE

LIQUIDITY
AVAILABLE

PERCEIVED RISK &
GENERALIZED FEAR

Source: Alan E. Grunewald & Alex J. Pollock, "Money Managers and Bank Liquidy," 1985.

rapidly—it walks off the end of the plank. This is a recurring pattern at the end of bubbles, yet managers, investors, regulators, traders, politicians, and economists are nonetheless taken by surprise. As late as the first half of 2007, for example, the financial world was being treated to discussions of the supply of "abundant liquidity," a "global savings glut," or even a "flood of global liquidity," which would guarantee a strong market for risky assets. Many said that we had entered a new era of global liquidity. Limited imagination of the downside possibilities is typical of the credit booms that precede and cause the panic.

Liquidity crises do not last forever, although it seems like forever while they do last. Ultimately, losses are taken, risks reassessed, models rewritten, and revised asset prices discovered. A, B, C, D, and E get back to trading and lending. "Liquidity" returns. It was in the process of returning as debt markets calmed down and equity markets recovered, starting in the second quarter of 2009. Once liquidity fully returns, within a few years financial actors will take it for granted once again.

At a conference on the crisis in late 2007, an international economist intoned, "What we have learned from this crisis is the importance of liquidity risk."

"Yes," I replied, "that's what we learn from every crisis."

5

BUBBLES AND ECONOMICS: CONFOUNDING ISAAC NEWTON

Bubbles keep happening in part because financial experts manage to convince themselves that they have solved old puzzles and can predict the behavior of markets in the future, in the way that Sir Isaac Newton was able to predict the movement of the planets by formulating his laws of motion.

But the confidence of the financial managers, model builders, traders, and regulators is not warranted in the same way as was Newton's.

Consider this statement by Federal Reserve Chairman Ben Bernanke in June 2007: "The troubles in the subprime sector seem unlikely to seriously spill over to the broader economy or the financial system."[28] Two months later, the international financial panic started, triggered by the collapse of the sub-prime mortgage sector.

The following spring, in March 2008, Treasury Secretary Henry Paulson said, "I have great, great confidence in our capital markets and in our financial institutions. Our financial institutions, banks, and investments banks, are strong."[29]

Eight months later, he was directing a massive bailout of these same banks. Here is what he said then: "We are going through a financial crisis more severe *and unpredictable* than any in our lifetimes."[30] The remarkable change of view expressed in these quotes from Chairman Bernanke and Secretary Paulson is reminiscent of the saying attributed to baseball legend Yogi Berra: "Predicting is hard, especially the future."

Bubbles look different in hindsight than they do while they are happening. Looking back, bubble behavior appears stupid; nonetheless, while bubbles are under way, many very intelligent people get caught up in them. Remember Bagehot's point that it is not only "the sanguine and the ardent," but "the ablest and the cleverest the most" who participate.[31] Brilliant mathematical modelers and shrewd Wall Street bankers helped inflate our most recent bubble and then were dragged down by its collapse.

Judge Richard Posner, a legal scholar and commentator on economics, has written insightfully:

> The premise is that this [mortgage] debt was sold to suckers. But in fact it was sold to sophisticated investors. They knew a disastrous, nationwide fall in housing prices would make the mortgages packaged in these securities worth much less, but they thought, as did most of the financial and regulatory community, that the risk of such a disaster was remote. But risks that seem remote even to informed observers do sometimes materialize. Only in hindsight are they seen as inevitable, and the failure to have predicted them attributed to stupidity, greed and recklessness.[32]

What makes the whole subject of financial crises especially fascinating is that they are not created by stupid people, but by clever ones.

Three hundred years ago, among those entangled in the crisis of his day, the South Sea Bubble of 1720, was Sir Isaac Newton himself. Newton sold his original investment in the South Sea Company for a 100 percent profit, but when the price continued on up, he bought back in—and was stuck with a huge loss when the bubble turned to panic. Newton wrote in disgust, "I can calculate the motions of the heavenly bodies, but not the madness of people."[33]

Can we calculate the "madness of people" any better now? Our experience of trying to do so with mathematical models in the most recent bubble suggests not. During the rapid house-price inflation and accompanying over-expansion of risky mortgages, traders, analyzers of mortgage-backed securities, and regulators became enamored with these mathematical models of risk. How well did the models predict human behavior as the mortgage finance system changed, partially in response to use of the models themselves? Very poorly.

Did the models pick up the effects of short memories—of the inclination to convince ourselves that what we are seeing is "innovation" and "creativity" when in truth all that is happening is a lowering of credit standards by new names? Did the models show that what banks were counting as "profits" was the result of exponentially increased risk? Did the models adequately take into account the cumulative human forces of optimism, gullibility, short-term focus, the assumption that current trends will last forever, group psychology, and increasing fraud? Did the models keep up with the rapid pace of change in the very behavior that the models were supposed to describe? Obviously, they did not.

IS ECONOMICS A SCIENCE?

As James Grant observes: "In technology, banking has almost never looked back. On the other hand, this progress has paid scant dividends in judgment. Surrounded by their computer terminals, bankers in the 1980s committed some of the greatest howlers in American financial history"[34]—just as they did again twenty years later, this time surrounded by vastly more computer power.

Using Newton's laws, the courses of the planets can be predicted with accuracy and complete agreement among experts hundreds of years into the future. The course of financial markets, on the other hand, cannot be reliably predicted for the next six, or even three, months. On top of that, financial forecasts are always hotly disputed among experts, who never agree on what is coming next.

So while economics aspires to be a science, able to make mathematical predictions like physics, in this it does not succeed—and neither does finance.

The great investment guru Benjamin Graham wrote in his classic book *The Intelligent Investor*:

> The concept of future prospects...invites the application of formulas out of higher mathematics to establish the present value of the

favored issues. But the combination of precise formulas with highly imprecise assumptions can be used to establish, or rather to justify, practically any value one wishes.... Mathematics is ordinarily considered as producing precise and dependable results: but in the stock market [or in the subprime mortgage market!] the more elaborate and abstruse the mathematics, the more uncertain and speculative are the conclusions.[35]

Fred Schwed so rightly observed in his wonderful 1940 book on investing, *Where Are the Customers' Yachts?*, that what everybody in financial markets wants to know is the one thing nobody can know: the future.[36] Alas.

However, there are two general things we can

BAD LOANS ARE MADE IN GOOD TIMES.

—*Former Chief Credit Officer, 1950's*

---

know about the future. First, the overall trend of an enterprising market economy will be growth. Second, there will continue to be cycles of good times and bad times, and the bad times will arise from mistakes made in the good times. From a financial point of view, the issue is perfectly summed up by the dictum of an old chief credit officer of the 1950s: Bad loans are made in good times.

History shows that acting on this wisdom is difficult. But remember the Biblical example of Pharaoh's dream, from which Joseph drew the correct lesson. He saved up some of the crops during the fat years to prepare for the coming lean years.

In banking and financial markets, this means that to be successful in making loans over the long term, it is necessary to build up reserves for future losses during the good times. Since the bad times will assuredly come, prudent bank managers look ahead to them and build up their reserves when they have the revenue to do so. The temptation, however, in good times, is to report the highest possible profits, pay big bonuses, engage in stock-buyback programs that deplete your equity capital, run up your leverage, and read your laudatory press clippings. Building loss reserves cuts into all of these enjoyable activities. But those who do not build reserves during the boom are candidates to end up in the government's clutches when the bust comes.

This was forcefully stated by George Champion, the former Chairman of Chase Manhattan Bank, when he recommended in 1978 that banks "increase the reserve for bad debts to the point of having at least 5 percent of total loans. This would not be out of line with the enormous losses that had to be written off in the last few years." (He was referring to the losses of the mid-1970s).

He continued: "Don't apply for privileges and be turned down in Washington.... You lose your strength. You lose your independence. Don't get in a position where you are going to have to rely on the government to bail you out."[37] Good advice!

A credit expansion in a bubble appears to generate huge banking profits. But a lot of these accounting profits are not real—they are an illusion created by the credit expansion itself. In recent years, the illusion has been reinforced by official accounting standards and regulatory rules, which restrict, rather than encourage, rational loss reserving.

So, to cope with the future, banks should build bigger, more old-fashioned loss reserves in the good times, as recommended by George Champion and by the book of Genesis. This would help our financial system and our economy better weather the next downturn.

6

DID THEY REALLY BELIEVE HOUSE PRICES COULDN'T GO DOWN?

Are You Missing the Real Estate Boom? Why Home Values and Other Real Estate Investments Will Climb Through The End of The Decade—And How to Profit From Them

—Book title, 2005[38]

You can see a picture of the housing bubble on the graph on the next page. Its inflation ran for over five years. Now, as I write in 2010, we are over three years into the deflation of the housing bubble. U.S. national average house prices have gotten back to their longer-term trend line, as also shown on the graph. As gravity pulls a thrown object back down, at least at this point, house prices are back their long-term trend line.

In one sense, the bubble was amazing: How could this really have happened? Don't people know better? Wasn't it clear well before 2006 that houses were overvalued?

Prices can go down as well as up. That is common sense. But participants in a bubble believe, and want to believe, that prices of the hot asset will keep rising. The poet Edna St. Vincent Millay was talking about physical attraction in the following verses, but they can equally apply to the emotions of investing and borrowing for speculative capital gains:

> So subtly is the fume of life designed
> To clarify the pulse and cloud the mind.[39]

The speculative pulse is likely to speed up, and the mind to become especially clouded, in crowds. We have noted that James Grant, that astute and acerbic chronicler of the foibles of financial markets, argued that "in order to create a really big asset price bubble...a critical mass of human beings is all that's required."[40] But what about the financial professionals? Did the professionals who

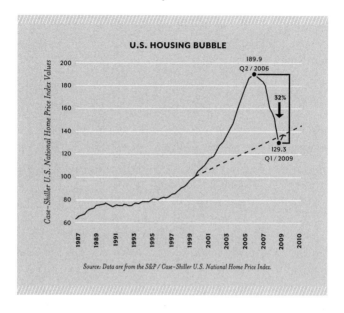

U.S. HOUSING BUBBLE

189.9
Q2 / 2006

32%

129.3
Q1 / 2009

Case-Shiller U.S. National Home Price Index Values

1987 1989 1991 1993 1995 1997 1999 2001 2003 2005 2007 2009 2010

Source: Data are from the S&P / Case-Shiller U.S. National Home Price Index.

made the loans, or the ones who packaged the loans into securities and sold them on the financial markets, or the investors who bought those securities believe that house prices could not go down? Even more important, did the credit-rating agencies who were paid to analyze those securities believe it?[41]

These rating agencies were expected to be aware of the various risks that might undermine the value of mortgage-backed securities, since their whole reason for being is to assess the quality of debt. But even these seasoned professionals failed to see the coming drop in housing prices. How did that happen?

The professionals were well aware that over the preceding decades there had been notable housing and mortgage busts, with house prices in formerly hot markets falling, followed by high defaults and large losses on mortgage loans. These occurred in Texas and the other "oil patch" states after the implosion of the oil bubble of the 1970s and early 1980s, in New England after the end of its 1980s technology "miracle," and in Southern California in the early 1990s.

In fact, the severe "oil patch" default experience became one of the key comparisons that the rating agencies used in analyzing the risk of mortgage securities in the 2000s. The professionals knew very well that the path of house prices is a key determinant of the credit performance of mortgage loans and the securities made out of them. They knew very well that painful housing busts had occurred in the past and assumed that they would continue to happen in the future. *But they assumed that any such busts would be limited to regional markets and would not affect the whole country.*

It was thought that a serious fall in house prices would not, and probably could not, happen nationwide and drag down the entire national average. The United States is a truly big country, with an even bigger economy, including a great variety of regions and economic characteristics. Many professional observers—realtors, bankers, financial analysts, investors, and credit raters—believed that the national home price average might stagnate for a year or more, but nearly everyone also thought that it could not actually go down. After all, it was commonly argued, this had not happened since the 1930s. So, even the mortgage finance professionals, by and large, thought that house prices would not fall on a national basis, let alone by 30 percent! But they did.

We should know from experience that many things once considered impossible have nonetheless come to pass. Afterward, we wonder why they were considered impossible. In the midst of the crisis and the bust, the recovery of housing, mortgage, and financial markets, the banking system, and the general economy also feels impossible, but nonetheless eventually happens.

7

A $5 TRILLION
GOVERNMENT FAILURE

Many factors contributed to the twenty-first-century housing bubble. But we have yet to examine in detail one key factor: government involvement.

The most important government intervention in the housing and mortgage markets, and arguably the biggest government contribution to the bubble, were the "government-sponsored enterprises" known as Fannie Mae and Freddie Mac. Until their slide into insolvency, Fannie and Freddie were usually, and correctly, described as operating a government-created "duopoly" in the secondary mortgage market. Between them, they controlled about half of the giant mortgage market and were and are among the largest issuers of debt securities in the world. Together, they owed or guaranteed more than $5 trillion in debt.

Fannie—originally, the Federal National Mortgage Association—and Freddie—originally, the Federal Home Loan Mortgage Corporation—were privately owned, for-profit corporations, but corporations chartered by specific acts of the U.S. Congress. These acts grant special privileges and advantages to each of these entities, which is why they are called "government-sponsored enterprises," or "GSEs." Estimates of the economic value of these advantages vary, but they are unquestionably worth billions of dollars a year to each. The most important advantage is that the government guarantees their debt. This guaranty was said to be merely "implicit," not legally binding, but it was nonetheless quite real, as events have demonstrated.

Fannie goes back to 1938. It was originally part of the government and was created to buy government-insured mortgage loans to boost mortgage lending and home ownership. Freddie followed in 1970, in response to the credit crunches of the 1960s, during which government regulation made mortgage credit difficult to get.

The federal government used to impose a ceiling on the interest rates that banks could offer to depositors—the notorious "Regulation Q." But interest rates naturally fluctuate with market conditions. When market rates would rise above the federal limits, depositors knew they were getting a bad deal and would withdraw their money to invest elsewhere. When this happened, savings and loan associations, then the main mortgage lenders, didn't have enough cash to meet the demand for mortgage loans. Mortgages therefore had to be rationed, making home ownership more difficult. This was considered an emergency, so to correct for one government intervention (Regulation Q), a second one (Freddie Mac) was created.

Operating their government-sponsored duopoly, Fannie and Freddie became potent economic and political powers. The financing advantages derived from their government advantages allowed the GSEs to grow to giants. Many people in Washington were in fear and awe of them, especially of Fannie, whose hardball political tactics were notorious.

EXPANDING "ACCESS" TO MORTGAGES: BE CAREFUL WHAT YOU WISH FOR

Fannie and Freddie both ended up being something never foreseen by their designers. While founded more than thirty years apart, each was established at a time when, for different reasons, mortgages were hard to get.

But, naturally, circumstances changed. In the opening years of the twenty-first century, mortgages were not hard to get. They were easy to get. Yet, Fannie and Freddie kept on expanding, in particular, jumping into hundreds of billions of dollars of risky mortgages as the bubble market was inflating toward its top. They ended up financing a big portion of the bubble's frenzy of borrowing and buying. Because of the implicit guarantee backing Fannie and Freddie's own obligations, the investors who bought their bonds or mortgage-backed securities knew they were covered by the government, no matter what risks or losses Fannie and Freddie might create for themselves.

The result? Both Fannie and Freddie went broke, and the taxpayers must pay.

THE GSE "RISK TURKEY"

In this context, consider the following quotations, all so ironic in retrospect:

> "Let me be clear—both companies [Fannie and Freddie] have prudent cushions above the OFHEO-directed capital requirements."
>
> —*James B. Lockhart, Director, Office of Federal Housing*

Enterprise Oversight (OFHEO), March 2008[42]

> "What's important are facts—and the facts are that Fannie and Freddie are in sound situation."
> —*Senator Christopher Dodd, Senate Banking Committee Chairman, July 2008*[43]

> "The U.S. government does not guarantee, directly or indirectly, our securities or other obligations."
> —*Fannie Mae, Form 10-Q, August 2008*[44]

> "We have no plans to insert money into either of those two institutions."
> —*Secretary of the Treasury Henry Paulson, August 2008*[45]

Shortly after these optimistic pronouncements, in September 2008, Fannie and Freddie ran out of capital and were taken over by their government regulator. The government (the taxpayers) became the majority owner of both.

In his incisive critique of Fannie and Freddie's actions and the ensuing bailout, journalist Sheldon Richman wrote: "The key to understanding the saga of Fannie Mae and Freddie Mac...is this: They were created—intentionally—to distort the housing and mortgage markets. Government planners were not content to let voluntary exchange...configure those industries. So... they intervened."[46]

That is an accurate statement. The ongoing taxpayer

bailout of Fannie and Freddie is, without question, a government intervention to save previous government interventions.

Fannie and Freddie failed in a way nobody predicted—namely from credit risk, which is to say, bad loans. Over the years, with hundreds of articles and speeches attacking or defending them, even their worst critics did not predict that bad loans would someday take the two mortgage giants down. But they did. The director of the agency that regulates them is now effectively their CEO. Making sure their foreign and domestic bondholders get paid off at par will probably cost the taxpayers over $150 billion—an expensive failure, indeed. As of spring 2010, Fannie and Freddie are a giant risk turkey, roosting in the dome of the U.S. Capitol. The members of Congress cannot escape its presence, but they do not know what to do about it.

8

THE YIN AND YANG OF TWO BIG BALANCE SHEETS

The bailout of Fannie and Freddie illustrates a law of government behavior: When government financial officers—such as Treasury secretaries, finance ministers and central-bank chairmen—stand at the edge of the cliff of market panic and stare down into the abyss of potential financial chaos, they always decide upon government intervention.

This is true of all governments in all countries in all times. Nobody is willing to take the chance of going down in history as the one who stood there and did nothing in the face of a financial collapse. As Chairman Bernanke said: "I was not going to be the Federal Reserve chairman who presided over the second Great Depression."[47] Put in their place, chances are that you—or anyone—would make the same decision.

In a financial panic, the universal cry is, "Give me a government guarantee!" To some extent, in one form or another, such guarantees are usually provided. Thus, we have the 2007–09 series of financial bailouts, starting with Northern Rock bank in England and proceeding in the United States through Bear Stearns, Fannie Mae and Freddie Mac, AIG, Merrill Lynch, Citibank, and numerous others.

Everybody, including all the government officers aforementioned, would prefer a system in which private companies take risks and then profit or suffer as the risks turn out well or badly. But when the bad outcomes threaten the functioning of the whole financial system through uncertainty and panic, the interventions follow.

One result of this is that the power of the government grows. This is a negative and relevant lesson from the sequel to the story of Pharaoh's dreams of the fat and lean cows. Joseph used the wheat he had so intelligently stored up to increase the power of the government. The Egyptians were willing to give up first all their land, and then their freedom in exchange for relief from the famine. "You have saved our lives," they said, "we will be slaves to Pharaoh."[48]

An excellent lesson! For when the government pays, it soon tells you what to do. Therefore, crisis intervention and government bailouts, even when judged inevitable, should be kept as limited and temporary as possible.

THE PRICE YOU NEVER THOUGHT YOU'D HAVE TO PAY

An old banker boss of mine used to say, "Risk is the price you never thought you'd have to pay." Four decades of being around credit markets have convinced me how right he was. However bad you may think the worst case could be, when the bust comes, it is worse than that. In this latest crisis, a great many investors, a large number of former CEOs, and many others have indeed paid prices that far exceeded their worst nightmares. Of course, this includes the taxpayers, who will foot the bill for all the subsequent government interventions.

Not everyone pays, however. The standard pattern of bailouts is to protect the depositors, bondholders, and other creditors of the failing firm, while punishing the equity investors. In other words, those who had lent money to the failed firm get protected. Those who owned the failed firm suffer the most. Thus, in the Fannie and Freddie case, for example, the government obtained about 80 percent of the stock and the old shareholders saw the price of their stock go down 99 percent, while the bondholders will get all their money back, under the so-called implicit, but real, government guaranty.

But shouldn't the lenders to failed firms have to share in the losses? Investments are supposed to entail risk, a chance of losing as well as winning. In principle, yes, investors in debt definitely should have to share losses, but government intervention usually means that they do not.

EVERYBODY CAN'T DELEVERAGE AT ONCE

One result of a panic is "deleveraging"—that is, firms try to reduce their debt and the ratio of their debt to their equity. One rapid way to deleverage is to sell assets and use the cash proceeds to pay off the creditors. The result is said to be a "shrinking" balance sheet.[49]

Clearly, any firm can shrink its balance sheet by selling assets to someone else. But is it possible for everyone to shrink at once? Imagine the combined balance sheet of all the financial firms—all the balance sheets thought of as one big balance sheet. How is it possible for everyone to sell assets at the same time so that this *aggregate* balance sheet can shrink? If *everyone* is selling, who is buying?

The only way for the aggregate private balance sheet to shrink is for another balance sheet to expand: namely, the government's. This includes the U.S. Treasury and government agencies of various kinds, including the Federal Reserve and the Federal Deposit Insurance Corporation (FDIC). In other words, we have a kind of yin and yang of two big balance sheets: the aggregate private balance sheet can shrink only by the expansion of the government balance sheet.

This is exactly what happened in 2008 and 2009. From July 2007, just before the start of the financial market panic, to the end of 2009, the Federal Reserve[50] expanded its balance sheet by more than $1.35 trillion, or over 150 percent.[51]

What is the alternative to this in a panic? According to Bagehot—who is also the father of central banking theory—there is none. Here is his 1873 description of the problem:

> In a panic, there is no new money to be had; everybody who has it clings to it, and will not part with it…. [Merchants] are under immense liabilities, and they will not give back a penny which they imagine that even possibly they may need to discharge those liabilities. And bankers are in even greater terror. In a panic they will not discount a host of new bills [that is, make new loans]; they are engrossed with their own liabilities.[52]

Therefore, in Bagehot's celebrated phrase, in a panic, the

Bank of England—or, in our case, the Federal Reserve—must "lend freely" to calm the panic. Both of them—and many other central banks as well—certainly lent freely from 2007 through 2009.

BAILOUTS

Not only the central banks, but also the treasuries of many countries, expanded their balance sheets to keep the financial sector functioning. The United States, Britain, Ireland, Germany, Spain, the Netherlands, Belgium, Iceland, and others all displayed the recurring pattern of governments using the public credit to offset the losses of financial firms.

As discussed previously, Fannie Mae and Freddie Mac were kept afloat on taxpayer capital and have been explicitly taken over by the government. They have essentially gone from being "government-sponsored enterprises" to government-owned housing banks.

Looking at the general pattern, governments typically go through three stages when faced with a severe financial crisis.

First, there is delay in admitting the extent of the losses while issuing public assurances. One notable example, often repeated by various U.S. government officials in the first half of 2007, was the phrase, "The subprime problems are contained."

Second, the central bank lends to financial firms as liquidity provider or "lender of last resort," as recommended by Bagehot. Lending, however freely, may not be enough, since it provides, by definition, more debt. If a bank's capital is gone, however much more you may lend it, it is still broke. What then?

The third stage arises from the irresolvable conflict between the public's desire for deposits to be riskless and the many risks that are inherent in the banking business. To combine riskless funding with a risky business is, in fact, impossible. Attempts to do so simply move the risk from the private sector to the government, i.e., the taxpayers. Thus, governments—responding to public fear, and officials' fear of the dangers of inaction— periodically transfer losses from the banks to the public, and money from the public to the banks—as has happened once again in the twenty-first century's bubble and crisis.

Thomson Hankey, a mostly unknown intellectual opponent of the celebrated Bagehot, made two basic arguments against government assistance to banks, as restated by James Grant:

> No. 1, moral hazard: Let profit-maximizing people come to believe that the Bank of England will bail them out, and they themselves will take the actions, and assume the leverage, that will require them to be bailed out. No. 2, simple fairness: If Britain's banking interest can claim a right to the accommodation of the Bank of England, why shouldn't the shipping interest, the construction interest, the railroads, and... the agricultural interest? Shouldn't all actors be

equally entitled to benefit by any favors?[53]

These are excellent points and questions, but as an empirical observation, the threat of financial collapse always trumps them. In the face of such fears, government officials always intervene.

BAILOUT HISTORY REPEATS

Two notable examples of government crisis intervention are the bailout of Wall Street investment bank Bear Stearns in 2008, and twenty-four years before, the bailout of the largest commercial bank in Chicago, Continental Illinois, in 1984. Though a generation apart, there are remarkable and instructive parallels between the 2008 and the 1984 events.

Both Bear Stearns and Continental Illinois got caught up in an asset price and credit bubble: With Bear Stearns, it was the great housing and subprime mortgage bubble of the twenty-first century. With Continental Illinois, it was the great oil and energy bubble of the early 1980s.

Both Bear Stearns and Continental Illinois had long records of success in financing the assets that ultimately led to their downfall, and both were considered experts in their markets. They both represent a lesson in the danger of sustained success that leads to overconfidence. Both cases involved fraud. Fraud in mortgage originations increased the losses in the subprime mortgage loans bought by Bear Stearns; fraud in the oil loans it bought from Oklahoma crippled Continental Illinois.

Both Bear Stearns and Continental Illinois were considered by government authorities to be too intertwined in the financial system to be allowed to fail— Bear Stearns because of its global network of financial contracts with other firms, and Continental Illinois because of the hundreds of other banks (both domestic and foreign) that had lent it substantial sums of money.

In both cases, all of the creditors were protected, and it was really the creditors who were bailed out. The equity investors, as is appropriate, took total (in the case of Continental Illinois) or huge (Bear Stearns) losses. The managements and boards of both firms lost control and were humiliated.

In both cases, the critics of the bailout argued that it would create "moral hazard" by convincing lenders that they could be less prudent because the government would protect them. This it doubtless did, but in both cases, government officials viewed the risk of a systemic collapse as greater than the risk of moral hazard. They always do.

TAXPAYERS AS INVESTORS

In 2008, the "TARP," or "Troubled Asset Relief Program," of Treasury Secretary Paulson, and similar efforts in other countries, focused on the government's providing new equity capital to troubled firms, and thereby to the financial system as a whole. TARP was enacted in October 2008 as a part of the Emergency Economic Stabilization Act of 2008. It had the problem that Hankey foresaw: Lots of people got in line with their hands out, including automobile companies.

The real result of all such programs is that the taxpayers are made into involuntary equity investors. How should they (we) be given fair treatment as investors?

In the aggregate, the investments the taxpayers are involuntarily making ought to have an expected positive return, in exchange for the risks they are taking. Secretary Paulson suggested at the time that the TARP program might make a profit—and as of spring 2010, it appears that at least the part of it represented by investments in banks has a reasonable chance of doing so. The government's stock investments have earned dividends. They have made profits through the exercise of options granted to the government.[54] In time, these returns may well exceed the government's losses from other aspects of the bailout of the banks.

A generation ago, the government bailout of the Chrysler Corporation did indeed result in a significant profit to the government. This time, the government extended TARP bailouts to two big automobile companies and, implicitly, to the United Auto Workers union. There appears to be no chance of recovering all the money spent on this part of the bailout.

To protect the taxpayers' interests as much as possible, any bailout should be subject to two fundamental requirements.

First: All the activities of the bailout should be isolated in a separate accounting entity. Bailout investments should not be mixed in with government entities, but held in a separate entity designed for the purpose. That way, all investments and other assets, all debt and other liabilities that finance the bailout, all expenses, and all income, can be clearly measured as if the bail-out program were a corporation subject to clear accounting rules. An audited balance sheet and income statement should be regularly produced. The cost or profit of the bailout could then be judged not only by the involved government officials but by the Congress and, most importantly, by the taxpayers themselves as investors.

Second: 100 percent of any ultimate net profit from bailout investments should be explicitly returned as dividends to the taxpayers, just as corporate dividends are paid to stockholders. Such dividends might take the form of cash or tax credits. This would be a well-deserved recompense to the majority of the citizens who bought houses they could afford, paid their mortgage loans on time, did not engage in leveraged speculation, paid their taxes, and then assumed all the risk of the bailout efforts.

In this context, I am always reminded of Aesop's fable of the grasshopper and the ant. As you may remember, the grasshopper fritters away the summer, while the ant works diligently and stores up supplies for the winter. When the winter comes, the grasshopper pays for his carefree imprudence. In a financial crisis, however, the government's investing and refinancing operations always bail out the grasshoppers by appropriating the resources of the ants. Prudence, moderation, and virtue are their own reward, yes, but there should be dividends, too, if the bailout does make money. The dividend proposal is based on the moral principle that we ought to do something for the ants.

9

THE GOLDEN AGE OF GOVERNMENT REGULATION?

In many discussions of the financial crisis, it is suggested that there used to be a "golden age" of regulation when regulation prevented bubbles, crises, and panics. Was there ever such a golden age of financial regulation? No, there was not.

For example, in the 1960s, as we have discussed, government regulation of deposit interest rates ("Regulation Q") caused two severe credit crunches—in 1966 and 1969—during which mortgage credit had to be rationed for lack of funding.

In the mid-1970s, lending by the highly regulated commercial banks created a bubble followed by a massive bust in loans to real estate investment trusts ("REITs"). As previously noted, the Senate Banking Committee held hearings to investigate whether the entire commercial banking system was insolvent.

Historically, savings and loans were the most intensely regulated of financial institutions. The result? By 1979, by following their mortgage lending regulatory requirements, the industry as a whole was insolvent, if measured by the market values of their loans.[55] Over the next decade, with guidance and constant intervention by the Federal Home Loan Bank Board, the savings and loan industry's regulator, the insolvency grew worse and worse until it ended in final collapse—followed by a bailout in 1989.

What about the regulated commercial banks? In the 1980s and early 1990s, more than 1,500 commercial banks failed. Many of them suffered massive losses from loans to developing counties ("less developed countries" or "LDCs" in the jargon of the time); these loans had previously been cheered as a big success called "petro-dollar recycling." Many other banks lost vast amounts of money on loans to finance energy projects and commercial real estate. All of these loans were on the balance sheets of the intensely regulated commercial banks, and heavy regulation did not prevent any of the losses.

In the normal political reaction, Congress passed three new laws: the Financial Institutions Reform, Recovery and Enforcement Act of 1989; the Federal Deposit Insurance Corporation Improvement Act of 1991; and the Housing and Community Development Act of 1992. These actions, government officials said, would guarantee that such financial crises could never happen again.

In 1993, following this reformist legislation, the financial historian Bernard Shull insightfully wrote:

> Comprehensive banking reform, traditionally including augmented and improved supervision, has typically evoked a transcendent, and in retrospect, unwarranted optimism.... Confronting the S&L disaster with yet another comprehensive reform...the Secretary of the Treasury proclaimed "two watchwords guided us as we undertook to solve this problem: Never Again."[56]

Yet, a massive crisis has happened again anyway. In the meantime, in 2002, following accounting scandals, Congress also imposed the infamously onerous and expensive Sarbanes-Oxley Act to manage corporate risk. Nonetheless, we suffered another financial bust.

Nor is this misplaced faith in regulation unique to America. In the 1990s, the British formed a consolidated financial regulator, the Financial Services Authority, or "FSA," to centralize all financial regulation. But they, too, suffered a housing bubble and a financial crisis.

In early 2010, the "great question of banking reform" is once again being debated. We are now in the political reaction phase—a lagging response that is the inevitable conclusion to any financial crisis. Politicians have an overpowering desire to show that they can *do something*: punish offenders, humiliate those who fail, increase regulation, create new regulatory bodies, reorganize existing ones, or, in the latest idea, address "systemic risk," an idea we will take up in the final chapter.

However, no matter how we organize any government activity (or any kind of entity), as circumstances change, it will have to be reorganized. The perfect answer does not exist. Whenever we try to engineer and control human behavior, those attempts at control themselves induce unexpected adaptations and reactions, in markets, but also in the behavior of regulators and politicians. Hence, every reform requires another reform to address the effects of the prior one—and on ad infinitum.

SENSIBLE IMPROVEMENTS

My point is not that no action should ever be taken, but that we have to be realistic about what can be achieved, and mindful of the unforeseeable consequences of all interventions. Sensible improvements are possible, provided we don't expect too much from regulation.

Here are four suggestions for fundamental improvements:

A. Loans should become more conservative as asset prices rise. As asset prices rise in a boom, more borrowing seems better to buyers of the asset, and more leverage seems better to financial firms. Profits get (temporarily) bigger for both lenders and borrowers. Lenders and investors grow more confident. Risk seems to be decreasing, but in fact it is increasing. One way to constrain lending from inadvertently fueling a bubble is for lenders to lend less against the current market price of the asset, if that price is markedly rising.

One way to judge the riskiness or conservatism of a loan is by its loan-to-value ratio (LTV). This measures how big a loan a lender is willing to make, relative to the current market value of the asset in question—for example, how big a mortgage will be granted relative to the current price of a house. Other things being equal, the higher the LTV, the greater the risk of default. In mortgage lending, this statistical relationship is particularly clear.

As asset prices inflate higher and higher above their trend line, the risk of their subsequent fall is increasing. In such a circumstances, reducing LTVs as prices rise makes obviously good sense. Nonetheless, the opposite generally happens. Rising prices correlate strongly with growing optimism, and LTVs tend to increase rather than decrease. In our most recent housing bubble, the problem was made worse by "innovative" low— and no— down payment mortgages, which meant extremely high LTVs. The term for this behavior is "procyclical"; that is, it exaggerates the ups and downs.

Countercyclical management of LTV behavior, which would mitigate the ups and downs, would be rational: Reduce LTV ratios as the price of the asset escalates, and thereby reduce the riskiness of the financial system. This is a worthy goal to work toward.

B. Divide Fannie and Freddie into two separate parts, so no GSE is left. As we have discussed, in their arrogant days, Fannie Mae and Freddie Mac made huge contributions to the inflation of the housing and mortgage bubble. This reflected their being government-sponsored enterprises or GSEs, with the government guarantee making possible the exponential expansion of their risky loans. Remember that the taxpayer bailout of Fannie and Freddie is a government intervention to save a previous intervention.

A GSE is the unsuccessful attempt to combine being part of the government with simultaneously being a private company. It is now clear that an entity can be a private company, with market discipline, or it can be a government body with governmental discipline, but it cannot be both. Fannie and Freddie need to stop trying to be both.

So, when the crisis is over, the for-profit buying, selling, and lending arms of Fannie and Freddie should be turned into private companies—genuine private companies, with no government advantages or backing—and made to compete like any other firm, sink or swim. Fannie and Freddie's other activities—principally, dispersing taxpayer subsidies for housing and providing non-market financing for risky loans—should become outright government functions and be merged into the structure of the Department of Housing and Urban Development.

Thus, no GSEs would be left.

THE PRIME VIRTUE OF AN INVESTOR IS NOT CONFIDENCE, BUT SKEPTICISM.

C. Drop the government's "confidence" slogan. One endless theme in public statements about financial markets is that the government should promote "investor confidence." But I suggest that a confident investor is a stupid investor.

The prime virtue of an investor is not confidence. In fact, it is the opposite: skepticism. From a macroeconomic perspective, confidence does not lead to efficient investments. Consider, for example, that in the 1980s, government-inspired confidence led the public to continue to make deposits in insolvent saving and loans, which allowed those institutions to continue their disastrous speculations. Later, government declarations of confidence made the world confident in the debt of Fannie and Freddie, which promoted highly leveraged and ultimately futile house buying.

The right idea is to help the public understand that skepticism, not confidence, is the key to sound investing. If they can help it, they should never let their skepticism slip while listening to the stories about how we are in a "new era," the TV and Wall Street pontifications, the (former) explanations of why house prices never fall, and official government assurances that they should be confident.

D. Study financial history. "The mistakes of a sanguine manager are far more to be dreaded than the theft of a dishonest manager," said Bagehot. Jesse Jones observed that "the wreckage of the banks which...had died of exposure to optimism."[57] The best protection against excessively sanguine and optimistic beliefs is the study of financial history, with its many vivid examples of how easy it is for financial actors and government policymakers alike to believe something that seems plausible but is dramatically wrong.

"It is necessary to...turn to those theories, the

classical, that do include sequences of prosperity and depression, or 'boom and bust,' as an integral part of their thinking," economist David Simpson has written. "The present boom and bust is not, as some would have us believe, a unique and unexpected event—a one-off. In fact, it follows a quite familiar pattern: in recent economic history there have been many financial crises"[58]—just as we have observed throughout this discussion.

We should consider a required course in the recurring bubbles, busts, foibles, and disasters of financial history for anyone to qualify as a government financial official or senior manager of a financial firm.

We might even require all such officials and managers annually to certify that they have re-read the following passage from Bagehot's *Lombard Street*:

> All people are most credulous when they are most happy; and when much money has just been made, when some people are really making it, when most people think they are making it, there is a happy opportunity for ingenious mendacity. Almost everything will be believed for a little while.[59]

We should all try hard to remember this when asset prices and borrowing are once again cycling merrily up.

10

TAKING RISKS, TAKING RESPONSIBILITY

When a bubble has turned predictably to bust, politicians naturally think about borrowers who are in financial trouble. They want to *do something*. They are much less interested in the vast majority of borrowers who faithfully make their loan payments on time and in full.

This raises a fundamental question about risk taking. Looking through the cycles, as a matter of philosophy, my position is that people ought to be able to take financial risks if they want to. It is not the government's or anybody else's job to tell them they are not allowed to. But when taking risks, they ought to know the nature of the risks they are taking and be prepared to live with the consequences.

Risk-taking is a central force in a market economy, an absolute requirement for innovation and for achieving the long-term growth that markets—and nothing else—can create. Without the freedom to take risks, there will be no growth.

Think about the risk of getting a mortgage and buying a house. It is an important risk. But relative to some other things we might consider—say, sailing on the ship that brought our immigrant ancestors to America in steerage class and launching into life in the new world, or my great-grandfather getting on his wagon and heading out to a farm in the wilderness—the risks we are talking about in a mortgage loan are pretty modest.

So, let us ask: Should ordinary people be free to take a risk to own a home, if they want to? Of course they should—provided they understand what they are getting into.

Likewise: Should lenders be able to make risky loans to people with poor credit records, if they want to? Of course they should—provided they tell borrowers what the loan obligation involves in a straightforward, clear way.

CLEAR AND STRAIGHTFORWARD INFORMATION

A market economy based on the voluntary exchange of goods, services, and money, backed up by binding contracts, requires that the parties understand the contracts they are entering into. A good mortgage system requires that the borrowers understand the key facts about how their loan will work and, in particular, how much of their income it will demand. The current American mortgage system, unfortunately, does not fulfill this simple requirement. Instead, it tries to describe 100 percent of the details in legalese and bureaucratese, with thick packages of forms in small print.

Most borrowers sign these without reading them, even without understanding the basics of what is in them, because they know they must in order to get their loan. Government efforts to require "disclosure" of all the details have resulted in very little useful information for the borrower.

In 2007, the Federal Trade Commission completed an instructive study of standard mortgage loan disclosure documents, concluding that "both prime and subprime borrowers failed to understand key loan terms."

Among the remarkable specifics, the study found that:

- "About a third could not identify the interest rate."
- "Half could not correctly identify the loan amount."
- "Two-thirds did not recognize that they would be charged a prepayment penalty." and
- "Nearly nine-tenths could not identify the total amount of up-front charges."[60]

America is about the ability to take risks, but it would be good to make that risk taking as informed and responsible as possible. Yet, when in 2009, the Treasury Department published a white paper to recommend creating a new regulatory agency for financial products, including mortgage loans,[61] the idea of enabling and building personal responsibility on the part of borrowers did not appear anywhere in the proposal.

One good way to enable personal responsibility, as well as to protect borrowers, lenders, the financial system, and taxpayers alike, is to have clear, straightforward, short-format information (so-called disclosures) about the loan that potential borrowers are considering.

In Congressional testimony in the spring of 2007, I proposed a one-page mortgage form so borrowers could easily focus on what they really need to know.[62] Something like that would greatly improve the way the American mortgage system works. A simple disclosure document

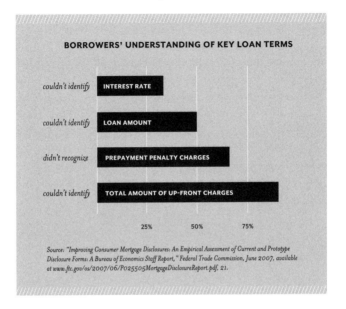

BORROWERS' UNDERSTANDING OF KEY LOAN TERMS

couldn't identify — INTEREST RATE

couldn't identify — LOAN AMOUNT

didn't recognize — PREPAYMENT PENALTY CHARGES

couldn't identify — TOTAL AMOUNT OF UP-FRONT CHARGES

25%   50%   75%

Source: "Improving Consumer Mortgage Disclosures: An Empirical Assessment of Current and Prototype Disclosure Forms: A Bureau of Economics Staff Report," Federal Trade Commission, June 2007, available at www.ftc.gov/os/2007/06/P025505MortgageDisclosureReport.pdf, 21.

would be most important for mortgages, which are the largest financial commitment for most households, but would also be valuable for other kinds of loans.

By far the most important purpose of mortgage information is to enable borrowers to make informed decisions about whether they can afford the debt commitments under consideration. This might be called the borrowers underwriting themselves. In the ideal case, the math to complete the one-page form and understand the relationships between debt commitments and income would be completed by the borrowers themselves.

The best consumer protection is the ability for consumers themselves to exercise personal responsibility in making informed decisions about how much debt they can afford and how much risk they are willing to assume. The most important reason to have clear and straightforward information is not just to provide understandable "disclosure," but to enable borrowers to act on it successfully. This obviously desirable step would help the mortgage finance system do much better in the next cycle.

11

CAN YOU REGULATE SYSTEMIC RISK WHEN YOU ARE THE SYSTEMIC RISK?

"Life can only be understood backward, but it must be lived forward."

—*Søren Kierkegaard*

Bubbles and crises affect not only specific investors, lenders, and borrowers, but the financial system generally. "Systemic risk" is a vague term used to discuss the widespread damage that overoptimistic expansions followed by panicked contractions can inflict. The term is not very well defined, but it refers to the possibility that the entire financial system could become unable to function through panic, illiquidity, and insolvency. It is frequently used to justify greatly expanded government regulation, but it is dubious that any regulation can succeed in addressing it.

A SYSTEMIC RISK REGULATOR?

Should there be a government agency which tries to act as systemic risk regulator? This is currently a question in political and financial circles. My answer is: No. This idea seriously overestimates the capacity of the human mind and the ability of human institutions—especially government bureaucracies—to foresee dangers and know what to do about them. As we saw in chapter 2, the ablest and the cleverest minds (aided by the most powerful computers and models) of the most brilliant economists and financiers cannot successfully predict the future. And no one can control it.

The distinguished economist Frank Knight observed that not only do we not know the course of the economic future, we do not even know the odds of future events—and moreover we *cannot* know the odds. As Knight wrote, "Uncertainty is one of the fundamental facts of life."[63]

"Economic forecasting was invented to make astrology look respectable," John Kenneth Galbraith is said to have remarked, and, as Alan Greenspan argued in 2009, "Regulation which fails is that which requires forecasting the future."[64] Remember another lesson of chapter 2: Economics is not science.

But we can distinguish between a systemic risk *regulator*, which I oppose, and a systemic risk *advisor*, which I favor. The latter might actually help ameliorate the inevitable cycles.

Consider this summary of our dilemma by banking expert George Kaufman: "Everybody knows Santayana's line that those who fail to study the past are condemned to repeat it. When it comes to financial history, those who do study it are condemned to recognize the patterns they see developing, and then repeat them anyway!"[65] This witty statement poses a disturbing and profound question: *Why* do we repeat them? Part of the answer is that the government, including, particularly, the Federal Reserve, is itself a key source of systemic risk.[66]

The history of the Fed since its creation in 1913 has been marked by periods of severe economic and financial stress and disaster, after which its policies have been revealed to have helped cause or make worse the crisis, and to have been inflationary or deflationary blunders. Among these mistakes are: the inflation and deflation in 1919–21; the collapse of the financial system and the Great Depression, including the Fed's 1937 "tragic mistake" of pushing the economy back into contraction;

and the Great Inflation followed by the stagflation of the 1970s.[67]

With the twenty-first-century bubble, we have another instance in which the Fed made big mistakes. "The U.S. crisis was actually made by the Fed," argued Columbia University professor Jeffrey Sachs and numerous others.[68] In 2002, one economist wrote as a joke: "To fight this recession, the Fed...needs to create a housing bubble."[69] Ironically enough, this is what happened—at the very least, the Fed made a significant contribution to inflating the bubble.

Of course, the Fed did not want a bubble, but there seems little doubt that it did want to promote a housing boom, which got away into a bubble. Thus, it kept interest rates extraordinarily low while the bubble was inflating, and it was very slow to recognize the depths of the problem when the bubble was deflating.

Nonetheless, some argue that the Fed should "regulate systemic risk." But why should we reward with even more power the same agency whose monetary policy stoked the housing excesses in the first place? As Senator Jim Bunning of Kentucky is said to have asked Federal Reserve Chairman Bernanke: How can you regulate systemic risk when you *are* the systemic risk?

Making this point about central bank culpability in a more academic way, economist David Simpson argues, "[T]oo great an expansion of credit will eventually be followed by a financial crisis and a possible recession.... [T]here were 38 crisis episodes between 1970 and 1999 spread over 27 countries. When credit as a percentage of GDP grew at more than 4–5 percentage points above trend, some form of financial crisis followed within one year on nearly 80% of occasions."[70]

Other governmental sources of systemic risk include GSEs, as discussed in chapter 7, and also federal deposit insurance. Government deposit insurance helps to increase leverage in the banking system by inducing bankers to take risks, because they know that their depositors will always get their money back, no matter what happens. A highly levered financial system will always have crises from time to time.

How low would leverage have to be in order to ensure a financial system that would never go bust? No one knows for sure, but it probably would require banks to have so much more equity capital than they do now that establishing such a rule would be a practical impossibility. Thus, the financial system will continue to run, even after whatever reforms may occur, at high leverage. And high leverage always poses systemic risk.

A SYSTEMIC RISK ADVISOR

Rather than a systemic risk regulator, we should consider creating a systemic risk advisor. One primary task of this advisor would be to supply institutional memory of the outcomes of past financial patterns. Its purview should be global. Its thinking and analysis should be informed by the financial mistakes and travails—private and governmental—made and experienced over the years, decades, and centuries. It should be overseen by a board with deep experience, have an insightful and articulate executive director, and a small staff with top talent. It must be free to speak its mind to Congress, the administration, financial regulators, the Federal Reserve, foreign official bodies, and domestic and international financial actors. It should be knowledgeable, imaginative, highly informed, and intellectually independent.

Such a systemic risk advisor should watch out, first of all, for the buildup of leverage, hidden as well as stated. It should also keep an eye out for signs that risky behavior is coming to be considered "normal." The advisor should be especially skeptical about assertions that we are in a "new era" to rationalize a bubble. "This time it's different" is among the most expensive phrases in the language. It must be aware of its own limitations in the face of fundamental uncertainty. It should remember that losses often turn out to be, as they have been in the current bubble and bust, vastly greater than anyone thought possible.

The advisor must seek to identify concentrated points of vulnerability to system failure. If such points develop, sooner or later they are likely to fail. Two good examples of such concentrated points of possible failure, which indeed failed at enormous cost, are Fannie Mae and Freddie Mac, as discussed previously.[71]

The systemic risk advisor must, at the same time, remember that risk taking is essential and that the failure of individual firms is not only necessary, but in the systemic sense, desirable. As economist Allan H. Meltzer says: "Capitalism without failure is like religion without sin—it doesn't work."[72] The main point is to keep our long-term growth trend—Adam Smith's "natural progress of opulence"—intact, with a hoped-for moderation in the cycles of over-optimistic enthusiasms and destructive panics.

Because uncertainty about the future is fundamental, financial mistakes will continue to be made. They will be made by entrepreneurs, bankers, borrowers, central bankers, government regulators, politicians, and, notably, by the interaction of all of the above. As Frank Knight wrote: "If the law of change is known…no profits can arise."[73] Likewise, we can say: If the law of change is known, no financial crises can arise. But the law of change is never known.

In enterprising and free societies, change reflecting uncertainty goes on, bringing the "natural progress of opulence" and the trend of greater economic well-being for ordinary people. Along with fundamental uncertainty also come financial cycles and crises. Knowing this, we should be better prepared for them and less surprised by them.

ENDNOTES

1 Paul Volker, "A Perspective on Financial Crises" (speech, *Federal Reserve Bank of Boston*, 1999).

2 Quoted in John Jay Knox et al., *A History of Banking in the United States* (New York: Bradford Rhodes, 1903), 194.

3 Quoted in Alex J. Pollock, "Collateralized Money: An Idea Whose Time Has Come Again," *Challenge* 35 (September/October 1992): 62–64.

4 *Report of the Comptroller of the Currency*, 1914.

5 Jesse H. Jones with Edward Angly, *Fifty Billion Dollars: My Thirteen Years with the RFC (1932–1945)* (New York: Macmillan, 1951).

6 Abram Piatt Andrew, "Hoarding in the Panic of 1907," *Quarterly Journal of Economics* 22, no. 4 (1908): 497–516.

7 C.P. Kindleberger, *Manias, Panics and Crashes*, 3rd ed. (New York: John Wiley, 1996), as cited by David Simpson, "The Recession: Causes and Cures," *Adam Smith Institute*, June 18, 2009, available at http://www.adamsmith.org/images/stories/the-recession.pdf (accessed August 17, 2009).

8 "World Economic Outlook: Sustaining the Recovery," *International Monetary Fund*, October 2009, available at http://www.imf.org/external/pubs/ft/weo/2009/02/index.htm (accessed October 13, 2009).

9 Carmen M. Reinhart and Kenneth S. Rogoff, *This Time is Different: Eight Centuries of Financial Folly* (Princeton, NJ: Princeton University Press, 2009).

10 Quoted in Alex J. Pollock, "Advice, Not Consent: A Case for a Systemic Risk Adviser and against a Systemic Risk Regulator," *AEI*

Financial Services Outlook (June 2009), available at http://www.aei.org/
outlook/100050 (accessed August 25, 2009).

11 Jerry Knight, "Banks Entering Era of Painful Change—More
Bailouts, Bankruptcies, Layoffs Likely," *Washington Post*, July 22, 1991.

12 Quoted in Pollock, "Advice, Not Consent."

13 Warren E. Buffett, Chairman of the Board, "2008 Letter to
Shareholders," *Berkshire Hathaway*, February 27, 2009, available at
http://www.berkshirehathaway.com/letters/2008ltr.pdf (accessed
August 21, 2009).

14 Adam Smith, *Wealth of Nations*, vol. X, edited by C. J. Bullock (New
York: P.F. Collier & Son, 1909–14), available at www.bartleby.
com/10/ (accessed August 21, 2009).

15 Pronounced "Badge-et."

16 Walter Bagehot, *Lombard Street: A Description of Money Market* (1873;
Westport, CT: Hyperion Press, 1962), 77.

17 Ibid., 127.

18 A broad term that covers all kinds of loans and debt.

19 Hyman P. Minsky, *Stabilizing an Unstable Economy* (New Haven, CT:
Yale University Press, 1986), 213 (emphasis added).

20 Ibid.

21 Simpson, "The Recession: Causes and Cures," 13.2.

22 Ibid.

23 Minsky, *Stabilizing an Unstable Economy*, 213.

24 Charlie Munger, "The Psychology of Human Misjudgment" (remarks, Harvard Law School, Cambridge, MA, 1995), available at http://vinvesting.com/docs/munger/human_misjudgement.html (accessed May 1, 2008).

25 James Grant, "Mankind's Bubble Gene," *Grant's Interest Rate Observer* 23, no. 21 (November 4, 2005).

26 David Ricardo, quoted in Bagehot, *Lombard Street*, 27.

27 Ben Bernanke, August 21, 2009, as quoted by Steven Sloan, "Bernanke Says 'Panic' Demands Action," *American Banker*, August 24, 2009.

28 Ben Bernanke, June 5, 2007, as quoted in Beat Balzli and Michaela Schiessl, "The Man Nobody Wanted to Hear: Global Banking Economist Warned of Coming Crisis," *Spiegel Online*, July 8, 2009, available at http:// www.spiegel.de/international/business/0,1518,635051,00.html (accessed August 12, 2009).

29 Henry Paulson, CNN, March 16, 2008, as quoted in *The Rise and Fall of the US Mortgage and Credit Markets: A Comprehensive Analysis of the Market Meltdown*, by James Barth, Tong Li, Wenling Lu, Triphon Phumiwasana, Glenn Yago (Hoboken, NJ: John Wiley and Sons, 2009), 1.

30 Henry Paulson, "Fighting the Financial Crisis, One Challenge at a Time," *New York Times*, November 17, 2008, as quoted in *The Rise and Fall of the US Mortgage and Credit Markets*, 1 (emphasis added).

31 Bagehot, Lombard Street, 77, 127.

32 Richard Posner, "A Failure of Capitalism," *The Atlantic*, June 17, 2009, available at http://correspondents.theatlantic.com/richard_posner/2009/06/financial_regulatory_reform—the_administrations_proposal.php (accessed on October 13, 2009).

33 Sir Isaac Newton, as quoted in Kindleberger, *Manias, Panics, and Crashes*, 34.

34 James Grant, *Money of the Mind: Borrowing and Lending in America from the Civil War to Michael Milken* (New York: Farrar, Straus and Giroux, 1992), 7.

35 Benjamin Graham, *The Intelligent Investor*, 4th ed., edited by Jason Zweig (HarperCollins, 2003), 566, 570.

36 Fred Schwed, *Where are the Customers' Yachts? Or A Good Hard Look at Wall Street* (New York: Simon and Schuster, 1940). 88

37 George Champion, interview, 1978, quoted in Grant, "Crooked Banker Found Hanged," *Money of the Mind*, 331.

38 David Lereah, *Are You Missing the Real Estate Boom?: Why Home Values and Other Real Estate Investments Will Climb Through The End of The Decade—And How to Profit From Them* (Doubleday, 2005). Lereah was the chief economist of the National Association of Realtors.

39 Edna St. Vincent Millay, "I, Being Born a Woman and Distressed," *The Harp-Weaver, and Other Poems* (New York: Harper and Brothers, 1923), 70

40 James Grant, "In Kansas We Busted," November 4, 2005, in *Mr. Market Miscalculates: The Bubble Years and Beyond* (Virginia: Axios Press, 2008), 154.

41 Ratings agencies are private companies that are hired by the issuers of various kinds of debt—mostly large bonds—to read the fine print; analyze the financial position of the issuing entity; and assess market conditions and the soundness of the business, project, or pool of assets that is the source of repayment. Ratings agencies—the most famous being Standard & Poor's and Moody's—then rate that debt according to their assessment of the issuer's likelihood to pay back what they owe in full and on time. Ratings range from AAA—the safest—down to D (though different agencies use slightly different symbols).

42 James B. Lockhart, March 19, 2008, as quoted in *The Rise and Fall of the US Mortgage and Credit Markets*, 173.

43 Christopher Dodd, "Late Edition," CNN, July 13, 2008, as quoted in *The Rise and Fall of the US Mortgage and Credit Markets*, 173.

44 Fannie Mae, Form 10-Q, page 95, filed August 8, 2008, as quoted in *The Rise and Fall of the US Mortgage and Credit Markets*, 173.

45 Henry Paulson, "Meet the Press," NBC, August 10, 2008, as quoted in *The Rise and Fall of the US Mortgage and Credit Markets*, 174.

46 Sheldon Richman, "Bailing Out Statism" *The Freeman* 59, no. 1 (January/February 2009), available at http://www.fee.org/pdf/the-freeman/122008freeman-richman.pdf (accessed August 24, 2009).

47 Ben Bernanke, quoted by Sudeep Reddy, "Bernanke Feared a Second Great Depression," *Wall Street Journal*, July 27, 2009, A3.

48 Genesis, Revised Standard Version Translation, chapter 47, verse 25.

49 A balance sheet is a statement of the firm's financial position at a given point in time, showing how much it owes, how much it

is owed, and how much it owns. When the total assets go down, the balance sheet is said to "shrink."

50 Specifically, the twelve regional banks of the Federal Reserve System. For more on the Federal Reserve, see note 66.

51 Based on calculations from Federal Reserve Board's *H.4.1: Factors Affecting Reserve Balances*, "Consolidated Statement of Condition of All Federal Reserve Banks," July 18, 2007, and December 30, 2009, available at http://www.federalreserve.gov/releases/h41/ (accessed August 18, 2009).

52 Bagehot, *Lombard Street*, 91.

53 James Grant, "Thomson Hankey Was Right," May 30, 2008, in *Mr. Market Miscalculates*, 29.

54 A stock option is a contract that entitles the owner to buy a certain number of shares at a fixed price at a moment of his choosing.

55 That is, the prices of those loans on the secondary market were below what the banks owed to depositors and creditors.

56 Bernard Shull, "The Limits of Prudential Supervision: Reorganizing the Federal Bank Regulatory Agencies," *Public Policy Brief* No. 5 (The Jerome Levy Economics Institute of Bard College, 1993), 15–16, available at http://www. levy.org/pubs/ppb5.pdf (accessed on August 26, 2009).

57 Bagehot, *Lombard Street*, 127, and Jones with Angly, *Fifty Billion Dollars*. 90

58 Simpson, "The Recession: Causes and Cures," 8.

59 Bagehot, *Lombard Street*, 78.

60 "Improving Consumer Mortgage Disclosures: An Empirical Assessment of Current and Prototype Disclosure Forms: A Bureau of Economics Staff Report," *Federal Trade Commission*, June 2007, available at http://www.ftc.gov/ os/2007/06/ P025505MortgageDisclosureReport.pdf (accessed August 24, 2009), 21.

61 "Financial Regulatory Reform—A New Foundation: Rebuilding Financial Supervision and Regulation," *U.S. Department of the Treasury*, June 17, 2009, available at http://www.financialstability.gov/docs/ regs/FinalReport_web.pdf (accessed August 24, 2009).

62 See Alex J. Pollock, "The Goal of Mortgage Disclosure: To Underwrite Yourself," (speech, Federal Trade Commission, May 29, 2008), available at http://www.aei.org/speech/28346; Alex J. Pollock, "The Subprime Bust and the One-Page Mortgage Disclosure," (testimony, Michigan Senate Banking and Financial Institutions Committee, November 28, 2007), available at http:// www.aei.org/speech/27144; Alex J. Pollock, "To Make Mortgages Fair, Keep Disclosures to a Page," *The American*, May 2, 2007, available at http://www.american.com/archive/2007/may-0507/ to-make-mortgages-fair-keep-disclosures-to-a-page. The "Pollock One-Page Mortgage Form" is available for download at http://www. aei.org/docLib/20070913_20070515_ PollockPrototype.pdf.

63 Frank Knight, *Risk, Uncertainty and Profit* (Boston, MA: Hart, Schaffner & Marx; Houghton Mifflin Co., 1921), 179.

64 Alan Greenspan, "Addressing Systemic Risk" (remarks, American Enterprise Institute, Washington, D.C., June 3, 2009), available at www.aei.org/speech/100052.

65 George G. Kaufman (remarks, Enterprise Risk Management

Symposium, Chicago, IL, April 15, 2008). Mr. Kaufman is a professor at Loyola University of Chicago.

66 To understand this, it is necessary to understand a little about the Federal Reserve, or the "Fed." The Fed is a central bank. It is a government entity, but one that operates in theory without direct interference from elected officials. Members of its Board of Governors are appointed by the President and must be confirmed by the Senate. Central banks like the Fed are established in order to take monetary and credit management out of the hands of politicians and put them in the hands of "experts." The Fed's role is in part to try to anticipate the right money supply for the economic times, and either expand it or contract it. It also has the power to set short-term dollar interest rates for the United States and much of the global economy. In tough economic times, the Fed may lower interest rates and increase the money supply, in the hopes that more available credit will spur economic activity. In boom times, it may to do the opposite, with the goal of curbing inflation. The Fed is subject to making serious mistakes in this role.

67 Bernard Shull, *The Fourth Branch: The Federal Reserve's Unlikely Rise to Power and Influence* (Westport, CT: Praeger, 2005).

68 Jeffrey D. Sachs, "The Roots of America's Financial Crisis," *Project Syndicate*, March 21, 2008, available at www.project-syndicate. org/commentary/sachs139 (accessed June 10, 2009).

69 Paul Krugman, as quoted by Arnold Kling, *Not What They Had in Mind: A History of Policies that Produced the Financial Crisis of 2008* (Arlington, VA: Mercatus Center, 2009).

70 Simpson, "The Recession: Causes and Cures," 24, citing D. Roche and B. McKee, *New Monetarism* (London: Independent Strategy), 33.

71 Others include the credit-rating agencies (see Alex J. Pollock, "Enhancing the Performance of Credit Rating Agencies Through Competition," testimony to House Financial Services Committee, May 19, 2009, available at http://www.aei.org/speech/100049); and the bailed-out, formerly AAA-rated insurance company, AIG.

72 Personal conversation with the author.

73. Knight, *Risk, Uncertainty and Profit.*

ABOUT THE AUTHOR

Alex J. Pollock is a resident fellow at the American Enterprise Institute. He joined AEI in 2004 after thirty-five years in banking. He was president and chief executive officer of the Federal Home Loan Bank of Chicago from 1991 to 2004. Mr. Pollock's research focuses on financial policy issues, including housing finance, government-sponsored enterprises, retirement finance, corporate governance, accounting standards, and the banking system. He is a director of the CME Group, the Great Lakes Higher Education Corporation, and the International Union for Housing Finance, and the chairman of the board of the Great Books Foundation.